Held Hostage

Held Hostage

A Story of Healing and Restoration

Aubrey Dawn Weinzetl

Held Hostage

By Aubrey Dawn Weinzetl

Published by Aubrey Dawn Weinzetl, Sioux Falls, SD

www.aubreydw.com

Aubrey.heldhostage@gmail.com

ISBN 9798987989302

Library of Congress Control Number: 2023905343

Editors: Cynthia Epp, Krystle Van Roekel, Bonnie Sandvold

Cover Image: Bonnie Sandvold

Cover Layout: Aubrey Dawn Weinzetl

Book Layout: Aubrey Dawn Weinzetl

Dedication

To my parents Douglas and Valerie, I am so very blessed to call you, my parents. You have been my support, role-models, and have shown me what it means to live out my daily walk with God. Thank you for always being there for me and not giving up on me. I will love you both always.

CONTENTS

Disclaimer: This book is based on true events. The names have been changed to protect the privacy of individuals.

(I changed the names in the book, first because I believe it shows honor to my ex, and second it felt weird using my name with a different man's name, so I decided to change both names.)

Prologue :

The Beginning

"I cannot breathe. The waves of depression pound me down, sweeping me away, battering me against the unforgiving rocks of dagger-like words. I dive deep, trying to pull myself out of the grasp of torment, but the words do not stop. I am swept away by the current of lies. I have lost everything. Who am I?"

"Please, Daddy? Please make this stop. I cannot do this anymore; it would be better for me to die than continue living this way. Please, God, make it stop!" I cried out in deep anguish of soul. The last fourteen years had taken so many twists and turns that in the end, I had lost myself. In fact, I had been assassinated— assassinated by the one closest to me, the one who was meant to forever protect me. My fairytale had turned into a twisted horror story.

My name is Ariella, and it means 'Lion of God,' but right now I feel like anything but that. I am thirty-four years old, but I have experienced too much in my short life span. My hair is currently reddish plum and shoulder length, I have crystal blue eyes, average height, and my skin is very fair with reddish tints. As a child I was always serious and withdrawn, wanting to be accepted and searching for someone to make me smile. My best friends were and are my siblings. Although I am a middle child, I took on many of the roles of the oldest child and still to this day walk in that role. My parents have always been a godly example to live by; they were and are a constant support. When I was young, I had imagination, passion, dreams, visions, and a calling.

Yet now, I'm nothing. I'm not worthy to even defend my own heart. I used to call God *Daddy*, but that all changed years ago. I no longer understood why He was silent, why nothing got better but only worse, and how He could leave me in this prison.

Somehow, I had become the unwanted, unloved, and abandoned daughter.

Fifteen years ago, I met someone I thought would change my life forever. Kanoa was tall, well-built from working out for hours everyday. He had dark black curly hair, midnight eyes that could kill with a single glance, and dark, smooth brown skin. He was easily admired by many. At first, he made me feel loved, wanted, and alive. Yet once we were married, how quickly the lies were revealed, and my world fell apart! His name was Kanoa, meaning, 'the free one.' I had no idea he would take this name so literally even after we got married.

This...this is my story. A raw and death-defying story, that I no longer have strength to live through. It is time for a shift.

Part 1:

My Past…

Chapter 1:

Year One of Marriage

"Where am I? How did I get here? Who...who am I? I do not belong here in this grave of death. I was meant to soar, to spread my petals open, and bloom into a flower that would reveal God's design for me. Yet all I see is death, decay, and darkness."

Kanoa's raised voice could be heard throughout the house as his anger intensified with each sentence spoken. "It's all your fault. You cannot hear from God. Stop trying to force me to love you. You cannot control me. Don't you know I married you so that I could do whatever I want to? I have the freedom to live the way I want and do the things that I want to do, and you cannot force me to stop."

Kanoa glared at Ariella with hatred, burning her heart into charred pieces. Ariella had only shared that she wished he would stop getting drunk because it scared her. Kanoa was a completely different person when he drank around family and friends than when he was home alone with her. Around family and friends, Kanoa would laugh, cry, talk about his homeland, or his favorite sport rugby. However, with Ariella the verbal assassinations would fly unrestrained, walls were punched, doors were slammed, and unbridled, unmistaken hatred flowed against her.

This was their first year of marriage, and the drinking had slowly started until it became a constant habit. Every time he would come home drunk, Ariella would fear for her life, her heart broken and battered. Constant terror and anxiety constrained her, yet no one knew. Ariella kept it inside, never breathing a word of how her life was falling apart. She had no idea that this would only be the beginning of living every day in a state of fear, anxiety, and brokenness.

"Kanoa, I am not trying to control you," Ariella forced herself to say calmly, holding onto her last ounce of courage. "I am trying to communicate with you how I am feeling and what your drinking does to me."

"It does not matter, Ariella, what my drinking does to you, or how it makes you feel. I will do what I want to do, and you cannot force me to love you." Kanoa stood unmoved, and there was no mistaking his threat.

The words hurt more than Ariella let on. It was not the first time he had said this to her. She knew that unless he changed, she would never truly be able to communicate with him and be heard and cherished.

...

Ariella still ponders to this day how she made it through that first year of marriage. Every time he left to go drink with family and friends, the fear would swiftly sink over her. There were many nights when she was left alone till three or four in the morning. That was when she was called to come pick him up. Somehow, she would carry him up to their apartment, take his verbal abuse and angry tantrums, then try and get a couple hours of sleep before work. She was the only one working, so to him it didn't matter when he would go to sleep. It was Ariella who carried the financial burden of the family, yet she lived in constant fear and lack of sleep. She was just waiting—waiting for the day he would react physically in his anger, that the verbal abuse would no longer satisfy him.

It came to a head on their one-year anniversary. Ariella remembers it like it was yesterday. It left a fear of drunkenness, which is one of the triggers that sets off her post-traumatic stress disorder.

...

Ariella did not know what to do. Kanoa wanted wine to celebrate their one-year anniversary, and there was no way to say no. She followed along quietly, hoping that he would keep his promise and not lose his self-control.

As the day progressed, it soon became apparent that his goal was to get completely drunk. With every glass, Ariella's fear continued to rise until it overflowed in waves, causing her to shrink inside herself.

"Daddy, I don't know how to handle this. I was never around drunkenness, and I don't know how to get him past this anger." Ariella was not sure what to do. She had no one to rely on. Her family lived hours away and Kanoa's family had no idea what she faced when he was drunk. That day, it only took a small moment before everything escalated. The apartment was littered with holes in the walls, the neighbor's door was kicked in, and Ariella was left shaking in fear wondering how to handle someone who worked out for hours every day.

In desperation she called his family only to find out most of them were out of town. Somehow, Ariella got Kanoa in the car, drove quickly to his family's house, and got him inside. A family member went back to the apartment with her, where she found the police waiting for her. Ariella calmly explained where Kanoa was and that she would meet them over there but needed to pick up a few items. The fear and dread would not stop. The unknown of what was to come hit Ariella full throttle. Quickly, they made their way back to the house, the police waiting to go in with them.

Kanoa would not settle down; his family and Ariella were concerned he would turn on them. The police gave him two options: sign the ticket and wait for his court date or be arrested on the spot. His family talked sense to him, and he signed, yet it was not over. Somehow, he had gotten more to drink. In anger, he threw the full cans against the wall. The explosion caused Ariella to freeze in fear as the words he screamed at her froze her heart. Finally, he went to sleep, and Ariella sat there for hours, broken, humiliated, and feeling very alone. Their first anniversary was left in shambles, but the lasting effect and memory has become a trigger that causes her post-traumatic stress disorder symptoms to occur.

The following day, Ariella and Kanoa received an eviction notice. They had three days to move out before they would be removed. A month later, they were moving back to Ariella's parents' house, hours away. Their rule was no alcohol inside their house. Ariella finally had a sense of hope; maybe without the temptation of alcohol, Kanoa would overcome his addiction, and the abuse would end.

...

Ariella still vividly remembers the fear, the pain, the brokenness, and the humiliation that were forced upon her. She remembers praying, crying out desperately for God to step in and protect her, but He was so silent. She wondered why He was so quiet, why He had abandoned her, and why Kanoa was not changing. No matter how much she prayed, cried, or sought God, nothing changed. Things remained the same and the verbal and emotional abuse did not end.

After moving in with Ariella's parents, Kanoa only drank when outside of the house and he never let himself get drunk. However, on visits to his family, he would drink too much, and the fear, pain, and helplessness always crashed over Ariella like a tidal wave. She did not realize she was on the path that would lead to her assassination. The path where she would lose herself.

Chapter 2:

Year Two of Marriage

"Two hearts that had become one were ripped in two in only a second. Fear, pain, and loneliness have become my best friends. Together we are traveling on a road through a wilderness that is meant to be my burial place."

"Jesus! Jesus! *Jesus!*"   Ariella's screams of betrayal, heavy brokenness, and devastation echoed throughout the house. Sobs wracked her body as she crumbled to her knees, barely holding herself up. The tears wouldn't stop. The gasping for air, the desperate cries leaving her own lips resounded around Ariella. The world had crashed and burned around her in a matter of hours, as his affair came into the light. The fingers of death weaving their way around her heart squeezed and suffocated her.

...

Year two of marriage was no better. In fact, everything became Ariella's fault. It was her fault they moved to her parents' house, her fault that Kanoa felt anger and resentment, her fault for the abuse because he said she deserved it. In Kanoa's flawed reasoning, this was tied to an incident that took place five years earlier when they were dating. Kanoa had confessed that he had kissed a friend in the kitchen. He kept saying it was just a joke and he just wanted to see how she would respond, but he continually brought it up.

At the same time this was going on, Ariella sent him a book of how they had met and instead of appreciating it, he was angry that she'd included both the good and the bad and he took out his anger on her. She did not realize then that he was a narcissist, who was trying to manipulate and control her. She was being groomed and she was not even aware of it.

Kanoa's constant jokes about other women and his lack of love and appreciation for the gift Ariella had so worked hard on made Ariella feel hurt and angry. She made a bad choice and cheated on him. However, her sense of guilt was strong, and she immediately broke up with both Kanoa and the other guy. She repented to God but could not forgive herself.

It was then that Ariella first experienced a deep depression that she could barely overcome. In fact, she found herself at a hotel, planning out her own death. For hours and hours, she saw the demons flying around her, screaming at her, telling her that she was worthless, that her death would please everyone. The darkest of weights fell upon Ariella and she cried silent gasping breaths. She can still feel the pain of her nails on her skin. Somehow, in the middle of the demonic battle Ariella heard the words, "Read your journal of what I say about you."

For hours she read and read till she understood that death would provide an easy way out but would cause damage to her family who had done nothing wrong. She knew that what would follow would be the hardest months to come.

Every day Ariella woke up and fought to get out of bed. She wanted to wear comfy ugly clothes, so she forced herself to dress up and put on makeup. She spent time with God, even though He felt so far away. She numbly went through the routine till she realized the depression was becoming less and less. She finally forgave herself.

Then, miracles of miracles, Kanoa and Ariella began to talk again, and then they started dating again. He constantly threw her mistake in her face. It was wielded as a weapon, one she could not argue against. She thought with time it would get better, and three years later when they got married, Ariella truly believed he had forgiven and released her. Little did she know that her mistake had been a huge blow to his narcissistic ego. Now, back in present time, it would all be revealed the day before their second anniversary.

•••

Ariella was on her knees in the kitchen as waves of betrayal and ravaging pain hit her chest. Confusion set in, and yet Ariella was not surprised because for months she had been sensing that something was not right.

In less than twenty-four hours, everything had shifted. She now knew that Kanoa could not be trusted, and she would have to be on guard with the women he would encounter. "God, I know many people in my situation would divorce, but I don't feel like I can. If we divorce, I will be judged, looked down on, all alone, and he wouldn't be in my life anymore. I want to give him a second chance to change and become what I believe he can still become." Without another glance behind her, Ariella took Kanoa back. Whether a mistake or not, it didn't matter anymore because the choice was made. Ariella had chosen to live without regrets. Sadly, Kanoa was only apologetic because he got caught. True repentance did not take place.

...

Ariella decided on a course of action, one that she chooses not to regret. Through it she learned what love truly means. Love is sacrificial! She still remembers the moment she found out about his affair, and how her breath froze. Her whole world collapsed, and she was so numb. Although Ariella had found out about the affair hours earlier, she chose not to respond till she had confronted him, and once it was officially confirmed everything hit at once. Since Kanoa's official confirmation was done on the phone, he never saw her brokenness. He never saw how, in that second, who she was shifted. She was heading further down the road of losing her life.

Chapter 3:

Years Three Through Five of Marriage

"I once thought that you would be my ray of light. But darkness was my only friend. I once thought you would protect me, yet I was forced to stand alone. I once thought change could happen, till I realized it wouldn't unless the person truly wanted to change."

"I'm leaving for work; you cannot force me to stay here with you!" Kanoa shouted at a quivering Ariella, who was trying to remain calm. "I do not want to be here at your parents' place. I do not want to be with you, and I want to find myself. I want to get healing and be healthy my way. I do not need you." Ariella sat in silence, taking in the true meaning behind the words. He had just betrayed her, and now he was abandoning her. Over and over, he would throw out the D word, *divorce.* She was trying so hard to fight for her marriage, praying without ceasing, but it was just one more thing after another. Living in fear, turmoil, and anxiety was beginning to feel normal. Every day he was secretive and if it was not the silent treatment, it was the verbal abuse. Ariella lost count of the times he would manipulate her into agreeing to things, by using divorce as the outcome if she did not comply.

"When will you come back?" Ariella asked defeatedly.

Kanoa responded triumphantly, "I do not know. Whenever I want to."

...

Ariella remembers how she changed that day of the betrayal. She lost her joy and depression was once again her companion. Although it did not reach the point of contemplating suicide, it was enough to interfere with daily activities. She no longer had trust, hope, or a sense of belonging. She was being abandoned. Kanoa had excuse after excuse, but the truth was he did not want her.

Ariella began to show unhealthy behaviors but had no idea how to stop. She checked his phone logs each month and each time she saw the number she felt sick to her stomach. Finally, after a year, she blocked the number without Kanoa realizing. The third year of marriage he was gone for six months. She never found out who he was with or what he was doing and had no way of knowing if he was being trustworthy. He would randomly answer calls and texts, yet Ariella was expected to answer immediately if he called.

The fourth year of marriage Kanoa was gone for nine months but visited every three months for a couple of days. The fifth year, he was gone for about eight months of the year.

•••

"Kanoa, I cannot keep living this way, being away from you. You said it was to get more money for your family, for us to save, and yet where has the money gone? We have nothing saved, your family loans are not paid off, and we are rarely together." Ariella was on the phone with Kanoa, once again begging him to come home.

"Ariella, stop forcing me to come back. I will do what I want to do." It was obvious that Kanoa was frustrated and angry at her. The situation was beginning to look hopeless. Ariella was hoping that if he came back home, she would be able to keep better track of what he was doing.

...

Abandonment does horrible things to one's heart. Ariella no longer felt worthy of being loved, wanted, or chosen. She lived with fear, anxiety, depression, and loneliness every day. Holidays were the worst. Kanoa seemed to purposefully make them bad. He tried to force Ariella to choose between him and her family. If she wanted both he would find ways to destroy it. He would sit there ignoring everyone, sending harsh looks in her direction. At times he'd make negative comments no one else picked up on. Other times he chose not to return for the holidays at all; he wouldn't come to birthdays, anniversaries, and other big holidays. Although holidays are Ariella's favorite and she loves family traditions, she ended up with painful memories of them.

...

"Ariella, knock it off, I am not in the mood tonight," Kanoa snapped, nearly shoving Ariella off the bed.

Ariella quickly left the room to cry; she was not allowed to show tears in front of Kanoa. If Kanoa saw her crying, he would immediately call her a baby or tell her that she was being immature. Weakness was not allowed. Kanoa rejected any expectation of being her source of comfort or someone to depend on.

"God, why doesn't he ever want me? To kiss me, or even be

intimate with me. His family always asks when I will give them a niece or nephew, but how do I tell them it is not my fault, because it requires Kanoa to be with me?" Tears of brokenness fell down her face unrestrained.

Kanoa always blamed it on being tired, but Ariella knew it was because he did not want her. She knew she was overweight but living with the stress and conflict in her life only caused her health to be so unbalanced that it was a struggle to lose weight. Working out had become another trigger to her because that is how he had connected with another woman. Kanoa had found another form of abuse and was now sexually abusing her by withholding intimacy for months, even years at a time. Kanoa knew of Ariella's desire to be a mom and knew that by withholding intimacy she would not be able to be one.

•••

Ariella still remembers how dark those years were. Married yet always alone. It was around the fourth year that she did something for herself. She went back to school. It caused many arguments with Kanoa, and he never supported her in it, but it was one area in her life that she could control. It was one thing she had for herself.

By the fifth year Ariella had developed responses to many triggers: Kanoa's silence, his sarcasm, his raised voice, his lack of response to message or calls, every time he left the house, alcohol, phone texts or calls he would not let her see, and any time she would approach for a hug or kiss wondering if she would be shoved away and ignored. In truth, there are many things that happened that Ariella has forgotten about just to survive. She has big gaps of memory loss and yet she can still feel how heavy those years were.

Chapter 4:

Years Six and Seven of Marriage

"Married, but we are strangers. Loving you, while knowing I am the only one in love. Standing on my own, while wishing to join arms with you and hold each other up. I am alone, utterly alone."

"Ariella, go make dinner. You said if I let you go back to school you would not let it interfere with daily life." Kanoa was beginning to sound annoyed.

"I know, Kanoa, but I just got off work and I have finals due by twelve AM. I still have so much to do, could you please help me out?" Ariella was desperately overwhelmed and hoped Kanoa would help.

Kanoa's gaze hardened, and his tone became threatening. "Stop throwing an attitude. If you do not want to cook, fine, we will not eat."

With a sigh of defeat and the nagging feeling of guilt, Ariella went and cooked. Two hours later, she brought the food down for Kanoa to eat. He was agitated, and Ariella hoped there would not be any problems.

Hesitantly Ariella placed the plate down. "Here is the food. I am going to work on my finals now and I will eat the leftovers when I'm done."

Without a word, Kanoa stood up with the plate, walked to the trash can, and dumped all the food into it. Ariella stood there with tears running down her face, completely shocked and crushed. Silently she walked out of the room, pulled herself together, and completed her finals one minute before they were due. When she had finished Ariella fell apart from the stress, lack of support, and the way Kanoa had treated her. A migraine followed, and in the wee hours of the morning Ariella finally fell asleep.

...

It took Ariella five years to graduate from university and every time she had finals or big tests, she knew to expect verbal abuse. In fact, she had learned that during holidays, when she would get sick, and when she would get her monthly cycle, she had to be ready for the abuse. It never ceased to amaze her how it always came during those times, and she would be forced to push it all away only to fall apart after assignments were completed. Yet because school was important to her, she fought to keep her grade point high. Years six and seven of marriage, Kanoa began to stay home more, but her happiness about that soon turned to dread because without him changing it just meant she never had a safe place to go.

...

"God, I'm so angry. How am I supposed to take his abuse, his hatred of me? It's obvious he doesn't really love me. I stay by his side, I watch what he watches, and I sit there waiting for him to acknowledge me and to open up and talk to me." Ariella sat in the living room crying out to God. Everything was coming to a boiling point and Ariella would soon find herself in a place of decision making.

Kanoa was in one of his moods again. The mistake Ariella had made ten years before had just been thrown in her face.

"Why would I want to be close to you or want you when you cheated on me when we were dating?" Kanoa pushed Ariella away from him.

"Kanoa!" Ariella said angrily. "That was ten years ago, before we even got married, and I have never cheated on you since, but you…you chose to have an affair when we were married. You broke your marriage covenant with God and me."

"It's your fault I did it. I should have just divorced you!" Kanoa shouted in anger. Within seconds, a deep anger surged over Ariella's body, and without thought Ariella slapped Kanoa on the shoulder as hard as she could. She quickly stormed out of the room feeling guilty.

A couple of weeks later Kanoa verbally attacked again, and this time Ariella slapped his butt as hard as possible before leaving the room. It was at that moment Ariella knew that she was crossing a line and that this needed to stop.

...

Even now, Ariella still remembers that anger and frustration she felt towards Kanoa. She was unable to defend herself, and she finally was pushed too far. It was around this time that Ariella read that people who are abused can become abusers themselves. She did not want that to become her story, so the next time the anger came, instead of lashing out at Kanoa, she walked up to the open door and hit it with the side of her arm, giving herself a bruise the size of a baseball. But she wanted to honor God no matter how she was being treated, and realized that hurting herself was not an option either.

From that point on, when Kanoa started his abusive rants, she would leave quickly and go sit in her car and cry out to God, go into the living room with music while silently screaming inside, or go into the bathroom and cry. She would only return to the room when she was utterly exhausted. By then, Kanoa was usually sound asleep like nothing had happened. In a way, even sleep was used as a weapon against her, because Kanoa knew that Ariella had been raised to handle sin, problems, and hurts before going to sleep at night. Very rarely would Kanoa allow the conflict to be resolved that night, knowing it meant she would not sleep well and the guilt of not taking care of the problems like God wants would make her restless.

However, on a positive note, Ariella was able to make it through and not become an abuser too. By taking her pain, anger, and bitterness to God, Ariella was able to forgive and not respond out of anger. She was able to keep her heart right and her conscience clear before God.

...

"Kanoa, I'm going to put my arm in the brace and have it rest here on the middle console, so be careful moving your arm around." Ariella had slipped and fallen four months before, and two screws had to be put in to hold the bone in her elbow together. It required months of physical therapy to get full motion and range back. During that time even putting up her hair, tying her shoes, or putting on clothes was impossible to do. That meant Kanoa had to help, and Ariella dreaded it every time because he would get angry and complain about it. He was angry because she was weak and could not force her arm to move.

They were sitting in the car at a gas station when Ariella reminded Kanoa that she would be using the brace and needed to be careful. "Okay, you should just force it to bend all the way and get it done with," Kanoa said in frustration. He got out to fill the car and Ariella once again prayed for patience. When the tank was finally full, Kanoa opened the door, sat down, and with force elbowed Ariella's arm in the brace. Excruciating pain hit Ariella and within seconds tears were pouring down her face. She tightly pressed her lips together, but the sobs still slipped out.

Kanoa reached over and hesitantly spoke, "I'm sorry, Ariella. I didn't mean to do that."

...

Ariella still remembers the pain from that day. At her next physical therapy appointment, the exercises were even more painful. She realized then that she could not rely on Kanoa for help. He refused to be there at the hospital for her surgery, so Ariella's parents went with her. He complained about helping Ariella, so even her dad learned how to put her hair up. Her dad took her to physical therapy, doctor appointments, and helped her with her exercises at home. She could not trust Kanoa. She always wondered if he would try to force her arm to do something it was not able to do. She began to truly realize that while she was married, she was all alone.

Chapter 5:

Years Eight Through Ten of Marriage

"Darkness surrounds me, telling me I have no value or worth. Yet a glaring hope is telling me to love myself. So, I am stepping out into the waves, and I am not sinking. Hope has come alive!"

"God, I cannot keep living this way. I feel so alone. Every day I come home from work, cook dinner, and then I wait for Kanoa to talk to me and acknowledge me. I feel like a dog waiting for my master to acknowledge me."

Ariella found herself once again communicating the loneliness she felt to God. Every day was becoming the same. Kanoa would ask about Ariella's day and say how his day went, but then he would immediately turn on the TV. No more talk took place. Even if Ariella tried to share more, Kanoa only vaguely listened but never communicated further or acknowledged that he was listening.

...

Ariella remembers how alone she felt during this time. Always waiting for the day when Kanoa would finally talk to her, and she would be known. During this time, she was completing her last year of school and her sister was pregnant. She felt strongly called by God to leave her job of ten-plus years and help raise her baby niece and nine-year-old nephew. She started taking care of her niece when she was six weeks old, and for ten hours a day, Monday through Friday, she became Ariella's daughter, born from her heart. Her nephew inspired her to be stronger and firm in her decisions.

...

"Ariella! You are barely making any money! Everything I make goes to bills. You need to find a different job that pays better." Kanoa was angry again about the finances. It did not matter if Ariella was called and was being obedient to God. They could not help Kanoa's family as much or spend money on what Kanoa wanted, so Ariella was supposed to cave.

"Kanoa, this is what God has called me to. You know that we have been trying to get pregnant and it has not happened. This might be my only chance to experience raising a daughter from a baby onward. I need to do this!"

Ariella held onto the Knowing, but she knew it came at a cost.

...

Ariella remembers the many times she was told that she could not hear from God, that her calling to raise her niece and nephew did not matter, because all that mattered was having money. She had helped take care of her nephew since he was two. She never missed a class party or a class program and was also able to be the teacher assistant in his classroom in preschool. She picked him up from daycare every day and spent time with him till his mom got off from work. For seven years she had been by his side and was his stable security. Being with her niece and nephew and pouring love out on them was one of the biggest joys in Ariella's life.

Kanoa did not understand her struggle. Ariella longed to have a child of her own, but she always had a battle raging inside of her, wondering if bringing a child into this kind of marriage was right. Would the abuse she experienced eventually fall on her children? Would she be able to trust him being alone with their children? Ariella felt guilty for wanting a child in this kind of marriage. She felt broken, too, when every month her time came, and she had to tell Kanoa that she was not pregnant.

Ariella felt like a complete failure. Taking care of her niece, raising her every day, is how God used the baby to comfort her broken heart.

•••

"God, once again I come before you. I cannot do this anymore. I hate being ignored by Kanoa."

Ariella sat watching a K-drama all by herself. Kanoa had flown to his country to see his family. Since they could not afford two tickets, Ariella was once again left at home.

A sudden realization hit Ariella though. It was time to stop waiting, stop watching TV shows she did not want to watch. It was time to listen to the music she wanted to listen to and stop sitting there waiting to be noticed.

•••

Ariella remembers how everything changed that ninth year.

They barely fought. Kanoa's angry verbal abuse did not happen as often or last as long, and it seemed like everything was getting better. The truth is that, essentially, they became roommates, living in the same home. They did not argue because they barely talked to each other.

Kanoa watched his shows and Ariella wore headphones and watched her own shows. He listened to his music, and she listened to her favorite worship music or her favorite Korean K-pop band BTS.

There was no communication or relationship. Sex was just a tool to make a baby and had no intimacy or love in it. Every time after sex Ariella felt empty and alone, and she lost count of how many times she cried during it. Kanoa never noticed.

It was during the middle of the ninth year of marriage that Ariella began to change. God laid a group of boys, who would become brothers, on her heart, and she began to daily pray for them. She could not trust God for herself, but she could trust Him for them.

For three months Ariella prayed for her brothers, when suddenly, she began to see that she was changing. She finally was feeling how real God was becoming. She started calling Him "Daddy" again. But with the good she was flooded by pain, fear, loneliness, brokenness, hopelessness, and betrayal. As she drew closer to Him, the more she could no longer lie to herself, push down the pain and memories, and could only stand there as wave after wave of the truth of her life hit her.

God began to show Ariella a new ministry He had for her, and how her brothers would play a role in it. She remembers the day very clearly when Kanoa began to speak against them. Immediately in her spirit she said, "NO! I will not let you steal or take away my family and ministry." Her eyes were opened that day.

...

"I understand, Father, I understand that what has been done to me is wrong. I know that he has not changed. Today I have this weird feeling, this strange peace, that if Kanoa fails me again, I will be okay."

Ariella was sitting in the living room, Bible open, worship music playing, and praying her heart out. For the last two and a half months this was how Ariella had spent her evenings, and God was showing up. "Father, I see that there are only two options for Kanoa. Either he will get his act together, follow You, and win my heart back; or he will fall, whether by affair, divorce, alcohol addiction, etc. We cannot go on the way we have. Something is going to shift, but which direction only You know."

Ariella sat back and listened when God spoke very clearly: "Ariella, there is a shaking that will take place. Kanoa will be challenged and rebuked. You will be protected during this time; I will bring family to help. During this time, if you stay pressed into Me, you will stay standing in the midst of the shaking. Ariella, everything will change."

The waiting had begun.

Eight days later, Ariella and Kanoa were driving home after visiting family. Since Ariella was driving and it was late at night, and they still had three hours left to get home, Kanoa allowed her to play the music she wanted to listen to. To stay awake Ariella blasted BTS loudly in the car.

Kanoa began to mess around with the vehicle's GPS system, trying to get it to work. However, it would not do what he wanted it to do.

"F— F—!" Kanoa exploded in rage, swearing over and over, and screaming in anger. Ariella froze at the wheel. Immediately a state of panic and fear swept over her, and tears began to pour down her face. Inside she silently cried out, "God, I cannot do this anymore, make it stop."

Somehow Ariella was able to form words, "Kanoa, stop shouting and swearing so I can focus on driving."

"Ariella! Just *f—off!*" Kanoa shouted. With tears streaming down her face and shaking hands gripping the wheel, Ariella focused on the GPS and got it to do what Kanoa was wanting. By the grace of God, Ariella drove the car till they got to a rest stop.

Kanoa chose to drive, then. He apologized on the way, but Ariella was not present, her mind was escaping. They made it home safely.

The next day, Ariella was rocking her niece at her sister's house while her niece slept, when suddenly, there was a knock on the front door. Opening the door, Ariella's eyes met Kanoa's. A message resounded in her soul and a clear statement rose within her. "Father, it has started. Let's do this, God."

• • •

Ariella remembers the tenth year of marriage. She realized she no longer recognized herself. In other words, she was no longer Ariella. From all the abuse and trauma, she was diagnosed with post-traumatic stress disorder (PTSD). During this year though, she chose to fight for her calling, her brothers, and for herself. She would not let Kanoa take them away from her.

Kanoa was once again acting like he was single and chose to make decisions like he was. He had crossed a line with an acquaintance, and although it supposedly did not lead to sex, it was still a betrayal and showed how his heart had truly not changed.

Ariella still remembers the day Kanoa showed up at her sister's and the shift that began in Ariella's heart, because it was four days before her birthday. Yet, she had a peace that passed all understanding, and she knew that this would be a year of great change. So, Ariella seized her freedom!

Chapter 6:

Abuse and Post-Traumatic Stress Disorder

"You are not done with me yet. I see the future and it looks bright. Everything that was stolen will be Restored. My journey is not over, and Your blessings are being poured out on me."

In this chapter I will define the abuse and trauma I endured. I am only focusing on what I went through, but it is important to understand that there are many more forms of abuse and trauma. Many of you have your own experiences with trauma or abuse. I will also share about post-traumatic stress disorder, referred to as PTSD, and how it has impacted me.

Forms of abuse that I experienced

Grooming: "Grooming works by mixing positive behaviors with elements of abuse. In the beginning, all behaviors are positive. Slowly, harsh elements are added in amounts that surprise the survivor but do not push the alarm to a high level. Over time the inappropriate come to feel normal."[1] The goal of grooming is to get the victim into a position of accepting abuse. Narcissists practice grooming, and can use charm, gift-giving, gaslighting, secrecy, and threats as a tool for their means. A groomer understands what a victim longs to hear and uses their words to control the victim's thoughts. Their goal is to keep the victim focused on their own desires, emotions, and needs, at the expense of the victim's needs. A groomer finds enjoyment in causing his/her victim pain to increase their own sense of control and will keep the victim's mindset on doing whatever they can not to upset

---

[1] Michael Samsel, "Adult Grooming," Livejam NPC. 2022
https://www.mobieg.co.za/abuse/adult-grooming/

or anger the groomer.[2]

Verbal Abuse: Verbal abuse means name calling, criticism, insults, humiliation, and the blame game is used.[3] Verbal abuse is meant to destroy the character, the uniqueness of the individual, and assassinate them emotionally. Verbal abuse can be accompanied by physical elements from the abuser. They will use their body to portray control in their stance, by throwing or hitting objects, and using their face and eyes to glare as a show of intimidation.

Sexual Abuse: Always withholding sexual contact when another person asks for it, withholding affection as a tool of punishment, and making a person not have sex for months or years at a time are just a few examples of sexual abuse.[4] Another form of sexual abuse is using sex to control and manipulate the other party. (Although I did not experience this in marriage, I want to make note that rape can still take place within a marriage. A spouse does not have the right to force the other to have sex.)

Spiritual Abuse: Spiritual abuse takes place when the victim is ridiculed or insulted about their beliefs, prevented from

---

[2] "Adult Grooming," MOBIEG, August 15, 2021,
https://www.mobieg.co.za/abuse/adult-grooming/.
[3] National Domestic Violence Hotline. "Emotional and Verbal Abuse." April 17, 2022.
https://www.thehotline.org/resources/types-of-abuse/

[4] "Withholding Intimacy can be Abusive too," Domestic Shelters, August 30, 2017,
https://www.domesticshelters.org/articles/identifying-abuse/withholding-intimacy-can-be-abusive-too.

practicing their beliefs, shamed, or manipulated because of their beliefs, or when religious texts are used to make the individual accept the abuse.[5]

Emotional Abuse: Emotional abuse "involves creating emotional pain, distress or anguish through the use of threats, intimidation or humiliation."[6] It causes the victim to go to extreme lengths so not to upset the abuser. The abuser will use degrading comments to cause harm. The victim's achievements are joked about, and their self-esteem is targeted.[7] Guilt tripping is a tool used to cause the abused person to agree to things that go against their character, beliefs, and morals.

Gas-lighting: Gas-lighting is a form of emotional abuse. The abuser will lie, lesson an impact of a situation, or switch the meaning of something they say. A few phrases that are common in gas-lighting are: "… 'It's not that bad' or 'you're over-reacting' or even, 'I never said that'". The end goal is to create confusion, doubt, where the victim will feel at fault, crazy, and the victim will begin to question their own choices.[8] All of his mistakes were my fault. No matter what happened it was always my fault.

---

[5] "What is Spiritual Abuse?" National Domestic Violence Hotline,
https://www.thehotline.org/resources/what-is-spiritual-abuse/.
[6] "What is Abuse?" National Adult Protective Services Association, 2022,
https://www.napsa-now.org/abuse-and-neglect/.
[7] "Abuse and Manipulation Tactics," Women's Rural Resource Centre,
https://wrrcsa.org/education/how-to-hide-your-tracks-online/.
[8] "Abuse and Manipulation Tactics," Women's Rural Resource Center,
https://wrrcsa.org/education/how-to-hide-your-tracks-online/.

Abandonment: Abandonment is a technique that abusers find efficient because humans desire connection. So, when this connection is threatened the individual who is being abandoned will "...releases certain neurotransmitters and hormones, such as cortisol and adrenaline."[9] When little connection is being made, another hormone called oxytocin is depleted.[10] Oxytocin is a "feel-good" hormone, so reduced levels in the body cause the individual to feel down, lonely, and sad. The abuser now has power over the victim because the victim will do whatever it takes to feel good again, and the victim will accept all forms of abuse.[11] Sadly, for me, the threats became real. For a period of five years, my ex-husband would leave and be gone for close to a year at a time.

Trauma experiences I endured

- Anger, verbal abuse, and throwing of objects while under the influence of alcohol created an unsafe environment and caused us to lose our home.

- Affairs of sexual and emotional nature

- Abandonment

---

[9] Sharie Stines, "Emotional Abuse and Threats of Abandonment," December 19, 2017, https://psychcentral.com/pro/recovery-expert/2017/12/emotional-abuse-and-threats-of-abandonment#1.
[10] Sharie Stines.
[11] Sharie Stines,

- The forms of abuse grooming, gas-lighting, abandonment, verbal, sexual, spiritual, and emotional abuse were consistent through the three years of dating and ten years of marriage, creating a heightened sense of trauma. Also, the duration of abuse and constantly living in a state of adrenaline are the biggest factors to my post-traumatic stress disorder triggers.

What is post-traumatic stress disorder (PTSD)?

Post-traumatic stress disorder (PTSD) is very common around the world. However, before moving on I want to mention that there are many different health issues that come from abuse and trauma, so it is important to get the correct diagnoses from a professional. If you suspect that you might be suffering from PTSD, please contact your local doctor, or a counseling center that is qualified to give a diagnosis. I personally chose a Christian counseling center to ensure the counseling was consistent with my faith in God.

PTSD is a mental health condition. "…triggered by a terrifying event—either experiencing it or witnessing it." [12] Many individuals can overcome it quickly, yet for others, especially

---

[12] "Post-traumatic Stress Disorder (PTSD)," Mayo Clinic, 1998-2022, Mayo Foundation for Medical Education and Research (MFMER), https://www.mayoclinic.org/diseases-conditions/post-traumatic-stress-disorder/symptoms-causes/syc-20355967.

those who experience the trauma for many years like abuse, PTSD can last for years. The good thing is that there is treatment that will allow individuals to properly function and handle the symptoms.

Symptoms of PTSD

Symptoms can happen as early as the month of event, or they may come many years later. PTSD can cause the individual not to be able to function in family/friend relationships, daily activities, work, and even in social environments. The Mayo Clinic website lists the PTSD symptoms below and groups them into four categories: intrusive memories, avoidance, negative changes in thinking and mood, and changes in physical and emotional reactions.[13] What symptoms an individual gets can change over a period and everyone is different. I experienced many of the following symptoms as a result of the experiences I've described.

Intrusive Memories Symptoms:

1. Recurrent, unwanted distressing memories of the traumatic event

2. Reliving the traumatic event as if it were happening again

---

[13] Mayo Clinic. Post-traumatic Stress Disorder (PTSD). © 1998-2022 Mayo Foundation for Medical Education and Research (MFMER). https://www.mayoclinic.org/diseases-conditions/post-traumatic-stress-disorder/symptoms-causes/syc-20355967

(Flashbacks)

3. Upsetting dreams or nightmares about the traumatic event

4. Severe emotional distress or physical reactions to something that reminds you of the traumatic event[14]

Avoidance Symptoms:

1. Trying to avoid thinking or talking about the traumatic event

2. Avoiding places, activities or people that remind you of the traumatic event[15]

Negative Changes in Thinking and Mood Symptoms:

1. Negative thoughts about yourself, other people, or the world

2. Hopelessness about the future

3. Memory problems, including not remembering important aspects of the traumatic event

4. Difficulty maintaining close relationships

5. Feeling detached from family and friends

---

[14] Mayo Clinic. Post-traumatic Stress Disorder (PTSD). © 1998-2022 Mayo Foundation for Medical Education and Research (MFMER). https://www.mayoclinic.org/diseases-conditions/post-traumatic-stress-disorder/symptoms-causes/syc-20355967

[15] Mayo Clinic.

6. Lack of interest in activities you once enjoyed

7. Feeling emotionally numb[16]

Changes in Physical and Emotional Reactions Symptoms:

1. Being easily startled or frightened

2. Always being on guard for danger

3. Self-destructive behavior, such as drinking too much or driving too fast

4. Trouble sleeping

5. Trouble concentrating

6. Irritability, angry outbursts, or aggressive behavior

7. Overwhelming guilt or shame[17]

Intensity of Symptoms:

The intensity of symptoms will change. Stress can cause greater or stronger symptoms. Reminders or triggers can also cause symptoms to be stronger. Having multiple triggers with stress can cause the symptoms to be even worse.

Common reactions to trauma include fear and anxiety, re-

---

[16] Mayo Clinic. Post-traumatic Stress Disorder (PTSD). © 1998-2022 Mayo Foundation for Medical Education and Research (MFMER). https://www.mayoclinic.org/diseases-conditions/post-traumatic-stress-disorder/symptoms-causes/syc-20355967
[17] Mayo Clinic.

experiencing the trauma, and increased arousal (constant alert), avoidance, anger and irritable, guilt and shame, grief and depression, self-image and views of the world become negative, sexual relationships (numbness or unable to have sex), alcohol and drug use escalates, and communication changes.

Here are responses to trauma and triggers that I experienced and some that I still experience today.

List of Responses:

1. Hyper-Vigilance Suspiciousness
2. Loss of Emotional Control
3. Avoiding Places Related to the Event
4. Preoccupied with the Event and Inability to Recall All or Parts of the Event
5. Feelings of Hopelessness or Helplessness
6. Fear
7. Apprehension
8. Sadness
9. Low Energy and Headaches
10. Irritability
11. Alienated
12. Overly Sensitive
13. Memory Problems
14. Inability to rest
15. Weakness
16. Nausea/diarrhea
17. Sweating
18. Sleep Disturbance
19. Emptiness
20. Feeling Punished
21. Anxiety and Depression
22. Loss of Meaning and Loss of Direction
23. Numb
24. Confusion
25. Flashbacks
26. Spacey
27. Withdrawal
28. Hyper-alertness
29. Anger and Grief
30. Emotional Shock
31. Crisis of Faith
32. Isolation
33. Nightmares
34. Poor Concentration
35. Overwork
36. Thirst/dry Mouth
37. Rapid Heart Rate
38. Dizziness
39. Fatigue
40. Grinding Teeth
41. Doubt
42. Apathy
43. Chest Pains
44. Shallow Breathing
45. Easily Startled[18]

---

[18] Jim Norman. 2016 Eastern Mennonite University. http://www.emu.edu/star

5 Fs of Trauma Response:

The 5 Fs of Trauma Response is the idea that the victim's response to a situation falls into one of five categories. Some individuals can experience more than one category depending on the situation, trauma, and mentality. The concept comes from the Regents of the University of Michigan.

1. Fight: this response makes it look like an individual is misbehaving. The individual could talk back, become aggressive, defiant, and blame others.

2. Flight: in this response, an individual may seek to escape the situation unexpectedly, space out, appear to be ignoring others, be distracted, and miss class.

3. Freeze: this response results in the individual giving up quickly, zoning out, ignoring others, and becoming frustrated and overwhelmed.

4. Flop: this response is shown by being disengaged, no emotions, and missing class.

5. Friend: this response is when an individual has an unhealthy dependency on others, does not own up to own responsibilities.[19]

---

[19] Trails to Wellness. 5 Fs of Trauma Response. 2013 The regents of the University of Michigan. TRAILStoWellness.org

I personally go between fight and freeze responses when experiencing a memory or trigger. The fight response I usually experience is talking back, storming out, and becoming defiant.

When it comes to freeze response, I space out and become frustrated and overwhelmed. For me it depends on the individuals, the trigger, and where I am emotionally. If I am under stress and already struggling, then it takes longer to pull myself out of the 45 responses listed above. When an actual traumatic or abusive experience is taking place, I then respond with a fight or flight response. The fight response tends to come out when I am being triggered, and the flight response is shown by escaping from the person's or situations' space, spacing out, and being distracted.

In Part 2, I will share with you how I overcame, healed, and where I am at now. I believe that the tools and warfare that will be shared will also help you heal, grow, and overcome. So come along on this amazing journey that only God could design.

Part 2:

…Won't Hold Me Hostage

Chapter 7:

Healing and Restoration

"A new day is here. A new door has opened. I live with wonder and excitement at what God will bring my way. Today is the day of victory."

I still remember the unbelievable, insane, and unexplainable peace I had when my ex-husband's infidelity was revealed. For one month we stayed together, but it was so hard. I would come home from work, cook, eat with him, and then I would go to the living room and spend time with God till about 11pm or 12am. I would finally go into our room, but sleep was restless, because I was constantly aware of the space between us and did not want to be touched by him. At 3am he would get up and get ready for the gym, so I would go into the living room and spend time with God. The whole month, I was blessed when I could get even five hours of sleep.

At the very beginning of that month, I had a realization that forever changed the direction of my life. You are probably wondering what that could be, what could radically change everything, and I will gladly share it.

When someone looks at me, I do not want them to see someone who was abused (broken), I do not want them to see a survivor (still carrying baggage), but someone who thrives (favored and blessed).

I will not choose the title of abused. I will not choose the title of survivor and always live in the mentality of survivor-mode. NO! I choose the title of thriving, favored, freed, and restored. Yes, it is true that I have PTSD, but my goal is to get to a place where I overcome it; and even if there is a little bit still there later, that it will not have control over me, nor the power to hold me hostage.

This mindset changed my perspective on all that I had endured and where I wanted to go. Although I still lived with my ex-husband, every evening and morning I would press into God. I would allow Him to bring back the trauma and the memories, and I would not run from them. I would feel all of them. I refused to push the emotions and feelings down, and instead I began to focus on the root problem those memories, trauma, and abuse caused. Once the root was realized, I then prayed for hours over it, found scripture verses that addressed it, and listened to what God had to say about it.

I also began to take my responses to the trauma, triggers, and memories to God. When I wanted to check my ex-husband's phone or follow him to see who he would meet, I realized that this aggressive drive or hypervigilance or suspiciousness was due to PTSD. I would work in the opposite spirit. I would pray through it and release that control to God, and soon I found victory in that area. It was during this time of praying and sharing, that truth and understanding began to be revealed.

At the beginning of the year the Lord had given me a chapter from the Bible for that year, Psalm 91 (NIV).

Psalm 91

[1] Whoever dwells in the shelter of the Most High
will rest in the shadow of the Almighty.
[2] I will say of the Lord, "He is my refuge and my fortress,
my God, in whom I trust."

[3] Surely he will save you
from the fowler's snare
and from the deadly pestilence.

[4] He will cover you with his feathers,
and under his wings you will find refuge;
his faithfulness will be your shield and rampart.
[5] You will not fear the terror of night,
nor the arrow that flies by day,
[6] nor the pestilence that stalks in the darkness,
nor the plague that destroys at midday.
[7] A thousand may fall at your side,
ten thousand at your right hand,
but it will not come near you.
[8] You will only observe with your eyes
and see the punishment of the wicked.

[9] If you say, "The Lord is my refuge,"
and you make the Most High your dwelling,
[10] no harm will overtake you,
no disaster will come near your tent.

¹¹ For he will command his angels concerning you

to guard you in all your ways;

¹² they will lift you up in their hands,

so that you will not strike your foot against a stone.

¹³ You will tread on the lion and the cobra;

you will trample the great lion and the serpent.

¹⁴ "Because he loves me," says the Lord, "I will rescue him;

I will protect him, for he acknowledges my name.

¹⁵ He will call on me, and I will answer him;

I will be with him in trouble,

I will deliver him and honor him.

¹⁶ With long life I will satisfy him

and show him my salvation."

This chapter was given to me December 31, 2020, and after my ex-husband's improper behavior with an acquaintance came into light, God would remind me of these verses in the most unique ways. I learned to look for the details, to see what God was saying. Friends would send me that chapter because God had told them to share it with me. Once I was driving and the license plate in front of me was Psalm 91.

I was amazed at the people God brought into my life during this time. I had my parents, my siblings, aunts, cousin, friends, and my brothers. I was able to speak honestly to them about everything, and they would pray for me, check up on me, listen to me, and encourage me on this journey.

It's amazing how the truth sets you free. For me, I was questioning my beauty and my worth, but then God showed me that my ex-husband had groomed me, that my confidence had been undermined for years. When we met, he acted completely different, but through months and years he slowly began to control what information I shared with others, that I took responsibility for all his mistakes, and that I was always wrong. Not only that, but there was an age-pattern to the other women he had crossed the line with; the ones I knew about were 19, which is also the age I was when we met. That realization set me free. It had nothing to do with me, my looks, or my heart, because the problem was within my ex-husband's spiritual heart.

At that time, I was struggling to decide if I had enough reason to divorce him. I know that sounds crazy but breaking free from his control and manipulation was hard. I had grown so used to the routine that not cooking dinner, not answering his calls and texts right away, and not acting like everything was okay had made me feel horrible and extremely guilty. When I realized I felt guilty for these things, I realized I had plenty of reason to divorce and that I had given him ten years of chances to change, so I had no regrets. I still remember how he would try to get me to give him another chance. I found it very enlightening when he said, "I am praying to see what God would want me to confess to you, and if there is anything I have forgotten."

Another area that I had to deal with that month was grieving my expectations for the marriage and what it could have been. Questions played in my mind: why could he not change? Why has he never chosen me? Why am I back here? However, soon my thoughts would shift to these: I cannot sacrifice myself anymore. I have laid down my beliefs, my desires, and who I am to cater to him in the hopes that he would change. All I have ever wanted was to be loved, treasured, and taken care of. The marriage was so lonely; I was constantly on edge, always having to be strong and yet always broken. I needed more than that. I had nothing left to give to the marriage.

During this time, God constantly spoke to me concerning who I really am. I am chosen. I'm His royal daughter, I'm His warrior, and I am not alone. In return I began to speak forth who God is and who He is to me. He is faithful, my healer, my Father, my protector, my comforter, my strength, my redeemer, my restorer, my beloved, etc. The more He claimed over me and the more I declared who He is, the more my heart healed, and I experienced His joy.

I continued to pray for others during this time: my family, my brothers, my friends, for the remnant, and for the nations. I also started fasting, praying, and giving. Every other month for two days I would fast and pray for others and for myself. The weeks leading up to each weekend were some of the roughest weeks of spiritual warfare, but at the end of the two days God would show up in big and powerful ways. To this day, I am continuing to tithe and give, pray, and fast, because when you are applying all three truths, it opens heaven in ways only God can do.

A lot of truths concerning character, spiritual belief system, and lifestyle concerning my ex-husband began to be revealed. This information came from friends from my past that I lost touch which, because my ex-husband would control what I could share with them, from journal entries I had forgotten about, and information that came directly from him. A big example of this is when he officially confessed to sexual abuse by purposefully withholding sex for years at a time. With these revelations healing and the courage to say, *"enough."*

Towards the end of the month when I could not handle being in the same room with him at night, one of my brothers declared, "Let it *begin!*" Two weeks later we officially separated, and my ex moved out. Up until that point I was on a constant roller coaster ride of emotion. I lost count of how many tears I cried, how many nights I could not sleep. The day he moved out; a peace overwhelmed me. For the first time, I had a safe place to be. I immediately packed up his belongings and redecorated my room, reclaiming it as a place where I could go to relax and rest in God. I no longer lived on edge, in fear, or in brokenness. My ex-husband was gone, and I was now free.

I found that certain memories no longer held power over me. I began to experience freedom in my PTSD where symptoms were becoming less and less as I healed from the memories. I began to focus on how I could reclaim myself. On the day of our ten-year anniversary, I went and got four ear piercings because I had given that up for him. (I originally had eleven but kept only two.) I went and got contacts, and I began to dye my hair fun colors like I had always wanted to. I did red, orange, light pink, bright pink, bright purple, dark purple, and then black. I'm excited to try more colors. I started learning Korean, going for walks, and losing weight, and spending time with family and friends. I chose not to make extreme changes, because that can become unhealthy. I made changes that would cause no harm, no big life changes, and yet would allow me to reclaim myself.

During this time in life, I also found churches that were Holy Spirit-led, spoke the truth, and stood for Christ. Every sermon spoke to where I was at but also to where God was going to take me. I also listened to words from prophets, and they always lined up with what God was saying to me: time to let go, be healed, new doors, new beginnings, and a ministry God has for me. It helped me to focus on my healing, overcome my fears, and begin to walk in my new title.

A month later I filed for divorce, and two months later it was finalized. The next day, I went and got two more piercings for a total of eight. The number eight symbolizes new beginnings, and this number has become special to me, as well as one that God has claimed over me.

Between the day that my divorce was finalized and the day God told me everything would change, it was six months. In those six months I had completely changed, healed, grown, and began to walk in my calling. It did not take years for this healing to take place; miraculously, by opening myself up to God and giving Him the fourteen years' worth of abuse and trauma I suffered, He expedited the healing and deliverance. He said, "Enough; what Satan has stolen, I am giving it back to you seven times seven. A double, no, a triple blessing awaits you."

As I write this book it's been just over a year since everything started. I am healthy, I am happy, and I am safe. Every day is a new adventure with God, I am creating new memories and God is redeeming holidays. I took back my old dreams, the activities, and hobbies I enjoyed, and my relationship with God and my calling.

In the next chapter I will share the steps and keys I used to heal, to grow, and to overcome.

Chapter 8:

Steps and Keys for Healing

"Every Step led to a new thing. Every key took me deeper into freedom. I am not afraid, for I am strong and courageous. Today I stand firm, while actively waiting for each step to be made known. Yes, today is the day where everything changes."

In this chapter I want to share with you steps and keys that I implemented in life to get the healing and freedom I am experiencing today. These tools where given to me by God, and throughout my experience He taught me how to walk them out. Each one is important and go hand in hand for true healing and deliverance.

Step 1: Your relationship with God must be a priority. You may be reading this book and have no relationship with God, you might even doubt His existence, you might have just a religious relationship with God. The relationship I am talking about is a covenant relationship with Him. It is pressing into His presence, worshiping Him, reading the Bible, and soaking in His Word. It is praying daily, speaking in tongues, and seeing His details every day. As I mentioned in the previous chapter, tithing, fasting, and praying have led to some of the biggest breakthroughs in my own life. There is a power that is unleashed when you are walking in all three, and God opens the heavens and miracles take place. It is allowing the Holy Spirit to do the work and speak to you.

A covenant relationship with Him is also about having the right foundation, based on the Bible and the Bible alone. The Bible talks about how we are to renew our minds and capture our thoughts to line up to what is good and acceptable and pleasing to God. Philippians 4:8 (NIV) says, "Finally, brothers and sisters, whatever is true, whatever is noble, whatever is right, whatever is pure, whatever is lovely, whatever is admirable—if anything is excellent or praiseworthy—think about such things." All other steps and keys are weak without this first step. You may get healed or get better, but to get to the place where you can live like it never happened and be restored back to your original design requires Jesus. Without God the Father, Jesus the Son, and the Holy Spirit, you will be limited and will not reach all you are called to.

Step 2: Acknowledge the trauma, abuse, sin, etc. I fought this for years. I did not want to associate myself as abused, because I would have to face reality. You need to acknowledge what you need to face, whether it's trauma, abuse, sin, or failure; whatever area is holding you hostage, acknowledge it. Hiding it will not help you, it just keeps you trapped longer.

Step 3: If you are in an abusive relationship whether family, friends, school, work, etc., GET OUT! Be wise in how you get out. If it's life-threatening, you will need to have a support system to get out safely or a place to go when you escape. Each state has a hotline, 911, churches, or abuse organizations. If you have safe family members, friends, pastors, teachers, or others, you can also get help from them. Regardless of what kind of abuse you face, you must make the decision for yourself to get out. I chose separation first to prepare myself for divorce, but not everyone will have that option. For me, it allowed me to get stronger and my resolve to become firm. You do not, should not, remain in a place of abuse. We are taught to love others as you would want to be loved; however, this year God has shown me that there is a balance. We need to love ourselves too. The Bible says many times how we are to treat our bodies because Christ is in us. 1 Corinthians 3:16-17 (NIV) says, "Don't you know that you yourselves are God's temple and that God's Spirit dwells in your midst? If anyone destroys God's temple, God will destroy that person; for God's temple is sacred, and you together are that temple." We also need to love others, both hand in hand, balanced, healthy, and honoring to God. You are special, you are loved, and you are not to remain in a place of death, but in a living, healthy, thriving life.

The following are keys that I utilized to heal, grow, and become healthy. They are the ways God used to restore me. The goal is to heal, be victorious, and walk in authority given to us by God. What follows is going to require active courage.

Covenant Relationship with God

In Step 1, I talked about having a covenant relationship with God. I cannot say enough how important this step is. The first month when we were still together but I stayed far away from him, I spent around five hours a day with God, worshiping, soaking in His presence, reading the Bible, and studying it, praying in tongues, spiritual warfare, and looking for His details throughout the day. I now try to spend an hour to an hour and half of uninterrupted time with Him. However, I am praying, listening to worship music, and talking about Him throughout my days. I love being close to God and listening to what He wants to tell me.

Choose Spiritual Support System

Be open to a pastor, counselor, family member, spiritual mother/father, or friend who can walk with you through this healing time. Choose wisely who these people are. They should be spiritually alive in the Lord, filled with the Spirit, and they should be ones you are safe with. Ask God to bring the right individuals into your life. Remember, bringing things into the light allows for healing. What is kept in the dark gives Satan power to hold you hostage.

Do Not Run from It All; Face It Boldly

Do not run from it all; face it boldly. I did not want to be held hostage longer than was necessary, so I chose to do it quickly. In the duration of a four-month period, every day I would allow memories of the abuse and trauma to come to mind. I would feel everything they brought and would not push them down. Once I recognized the true feeling I was experiencing, I would then dig deep to the strongman (demonic spirit) to see what spiritual identity I was fighting with and once the strongman was bound, I would deal with the stronghold he wielded. Many times, to bind the strongman it required me saying, "I forgive (name of person) who wronged me." I would let God show me how to heal from it, because some memories required different steps. For some, praying through it; others, binding the spirit; and still others, walking in the opposite spirit. This is when spiritual individuals came alongside to pray into these areas.

Get Involved

Get involved with a church that is alive in God and holds true to the Bible, where they speak in tongues, work in the prophetic, stand for justice, and truth, and do not waver to culture. I also was led to prophets who had been tested true and allowed their encouraging words to help grow me. (Make sure the prophets you listen to are true prophets; as we get closer to the end of ends, there will be false prophets.) It always amazed me how what I was getting from God lined up to what they were getting. God was confirming what He was saying. I also read spiritual books that dealt with healing, grace, warfare, and prophecy.

Walk In the Opposite Spirit

Walk in the opposite of how you feel. When healing, you experience many different feelings and emotions. One minute you will feel grief, the next anger, and the list goes on and on. Obviously, I am not talking about joy, love, hope, etc. However, even good feelings can lead you the wrong direction. Let me address the dark and painful feelings and emotions first: anger is not a sin, what you do with it can be. Negative feelings and emotions show us that we were hurt, that there are areas we need to forgive or even forgive ourselves. If they are not handled correctly, they can lead to further destruction. Every time I grieved, I took it to God, cried, and then prayed over it, asking Him to heal that area and then I released what I was grieving to Him. If I was angry, I would pray, and God would show me the root of why I was feeling angry. I would then pray, release the individuals involved, forgive them, and even other times repent of something myself. Anger and un-forgiveness can lead to bitterness, which has the power to control your thoughts, your heart, and destroy your good relationships. I want to share some personal examples of how I walked in the opposite of how I felt. I call it walking in the opposite spirit. We either are in God or in the flesh being led and used by Satan.

A. When I struggle with depression, I do not feel like doing much, looking good, or being active. I lack energy. So, I would get out of bed, dress up, see friends, go for walks, go to work, workout, eat healthy, and most importantly spend time with God. Another important factor was getting healthy. I am anemic (low in iron) and vitamin D deficient, and when I do not have enough it affects my health. In fact, when I have low levels, my emotions become extremely down and my body begins to ache; I feel fatigued, and my stomach begins to hurt. It is important to give your body the nourishment it needs, because it will also give you strength to battle depression by helping balance your emotions. When I walked in the opposite of how I felt, I created healthy habits that allowed my body to work with my spirit in communion with God's Spirit to overcome depression.

B. During the separation and leading up to the divorce, whenever I had anger at my ex-husband, I would instead respond in honor, with respect, and think about how I would want to be treated right now. Many of my friends said I was too nice, because I helped him learn how to do everything I had been responsible for in the last ten years. Did he deserve my kindness? No, but I can look back at those months and know that I walked in God. I was shining for Him. Before I move on to another area, I want to be clear on this: I did not reach out to my ex-husband unless I needed to, and when we met, my dad was always in his car parked close by in case I needed him. I prayed each time and if I did not hear a yes, then I would not meet him. For some, meeting your ex-husband or the person who hurt you would be extremely dangerous; for some who struggle with wanting to return to the individual, you should not meet them. So always pray and get advice from a trusted spiritual source like I did. The point I want to make is to walk in the opposite of anger, even when you pray, think about them, hear about them, or whatever God shows you, because He will lead you to areas to work on. I once had a friend ask me, "Doesn't that mean you are not being true to yourself and how you feel?" We live in a culture and world that tells us to do what we want according to how we feel, and that is how to live. But that is a lie! Our war is spiritual. We belong to God and so we do not live like the world. Anger, depression, bitterness, etc., if acted upon will hurt us in the long run. It will become my baggage, my open wounds for all to see, and I will live with them for a long time. As we walk with God in His Spirit, we must choose what is right and align our spirit with His. What is right does not change with our feelings and emotions. When we choose to walk in the opposite of the negative, we begin to change and heal, and we no longer have wounds and baggage, but hope, joy, and love. Take every negative feeling and emotion to God.

I have had many friends ask me how to implement this key in their life. To start off with here are some questions you can ask God to narrow down the root problem. What memory made me angry/hurt, etc.? Who am I angry at? Is there a true reason of why I feel this way? Where does this stem from (betrayal, unforgiveness, a sin, etc.)? This can be applied to any feeling or emotion. As God begins to show you, repent when needed, forgive when needed, ask God to cover that area, and then release that situation to God and take your hands off it. Continue to do this until it has no more control over you.

Before moving on to the next key I want to also talk about good feelings and emotions. During the healing process we are vulnerable and just because something feels good does not mean it should be acted on. Sin is still sin. Examples of how good can become sin: enjoying movies/books/tv shows and not spending time with God. Spending time with family and friends, and not spending time with God. Sexual and physical connections outside of marriage. Be in the Spirit, walk with God, and He will help you know how to live each day with Him.

Change Your Perspective

We are taught in our culture and world that only our own perspective, opinions, and feelings are right and matter. This is a huge lie. Our pasts, our traumas, our stories leave an impact on our brains. Our brains, our thought patterns, without us even realizing it, affect our view of what we see around us. When we walk wounded, we cannot clearly see what is surrounding us. The only thing that is right and that matters is God and His Word the Bible. Let me give you an example: My mother corrects me concerning something, and immediately I am triggered and have a fight response. Was my mother abusing me? No, in fact what she said was true, not a big deal, and I should have handled it differently. I am aware that my PTSD symptoms can hurt others, so I am working very hard to heal and overcome.

Here is another example: A friend is responding negatively towards me, saying that they feel hurt about something I never meant in a way to hurt. I stop to think about why they felt hurt, whether I could have done it differently with a better result, and then I ask for forgiveness. Come to find out this friend is hurting, they took what I said wrong, but they need some grace shown instead of judgement. Now reverse the situation and think about the times you were hurt by a friend/family because of what you were going through, and your friend/family never meant it that way.

Here is a big one: God, show me Your *perspective*! This is huge, because it will require you to get out of the way so that Christ shines forth. An example from my own life is with my ex-husband. When I asked God for His perspective concerning my ex, He revealed that it all came down to a spiritual and heart problem. My ex had un-forgiveness, pain, bitterness, and was walking in the flesh among other things. Did that make his actions, the abuse, betrayals, etc., right and give him an excuse? No, sin is sin. He had a way to freedom but chose this lifestyle of death.

We still have a choice: to obey God or to sin, and what we experience does not excuse us from blessing or correction. Instead of treating my past as an excuse, it allowed me to war in the spiritual realm and not against flesh and blood. Ephesians 6:10-13 (NIV) says, "Finally, be strong in the Lord and in his mighty power. Put on the full armor of God, so that you can take your stand against the devil's schemes. For our struggle is not against flesh and blood, but against the rulers, against the authorities, against the powers of this dark world and against the spiritual forces of evil in the heavenly realms. Therefore put on the full armor of God, so that when the day of evil comes, you may be able to stand your ground, and after you have done everything, to stand." I was able to walk in the opposite of how I felt during the separation and divorce because I knew my ex-husband needed healing and repentance. So, I released him to God, and rested in the knowledge that God will be my defender. Getting a different perspective led me to living each day aware of what was spiritually related, what others were going through, and how I fail at times to see the situation for what it truly is. Having the right perspective gives a boldness and authority to trample over Satan and reclaim what he stole.

Be Thankful

Be thankful! When going through healing, deliverance, and restoration, we can forget to thank God for all that He is doing, for the ways we have healed, grown, and overcome. We can lose sight of how God protected us, what has gone right in our lives, the blessings and favor He has given us, and we can even forget to thank Him for our very breath. Having a thankful heart during this process is a must. When we have a thankful spirit, everything shifts in our eyes. We can see what is truly going on. Negative emotions cannot remain in a heart that is thanking and praising God. Depression cannot remain when our hearts are thanking and praising God. We begin to see our situations through eyes of hope, trust, and faith. Thankfulness is a huge step to victory and reclaiming what Satan stole. Every day when I wake up, I tell God three things I am thankful for. Throughout the rest of the day, I am more aware of the good and will immediately thank God for it. Heaviness, depression, sadness, anxiety, and other negative feelings lift off me when I begin to thank and praise God. There is power in a thankful and praising heart.

Be Healthy Spiritually, Emotionally, and Physically

This goes without a long paragraph because it's straightforward and to the point. During times of trauma and pain and through the healing processes it is important to eat healthy, stay physically active, drink enough water, and get the right amount of sleep. For me it was at least five hours, but if I could get more then I would. Do not sleep your days away though either. Our goal is to heal emotionally, spiritually, and physically. Something else to keep in mind is that our bodies need vitamins and sunlight. As I've mentioned, I have chronically low levels of iron and vitamin D. When I am taking my iron and vitamin D, my body is healthier so when feelings that lead to depression arise, I can fight them off spiritually. When my body is lacking them, depression and those negative feelings will last for days. It is important that we become healthier in all three: emotionally (healed and no baggage), spiritually (close to God and walking with Him in truth), and physically (body working the way it is supposed to, the right weight and energy levels). It might be time to have a check-up and see if your body is missing some key nourishments, or even just start taking the vitamins, eating healthy, and being more physically active.

Be Aware of What You Allow to Fill Your Heart

Pay attention to what friends you hang out with, what television shows and movies you watch, and what music you listen to. Everything we put into our minds should be positive, Christlike, and edifying to God. The message should align with truth. I spend hours listening to worship music. For movies and tv shows, since I have PTSD and can also struggle with depression, I am very careful about what I watch. If there are affairs, abuse, violence, or sad or open-ended endings, I choose not to watch them. Before I watch a show, I read the recaps so I am prepared for what I will see. It helps me to keep my heart, thoughts, and body in the right spirit; it also prepares me to handle some areas that could be a trigger, and by knowing about what will happen I can choose to fast forward or not watch. Family and friends are important as well, so be wise on who you let speak into your life and future. They will either draw you closer to God and your promises or take you away from all that He has for you. Watch who you take into this new season. Be wise, be prayerful, and make decisions through the Holy Spirit.

Reclaim Yourself

Find healthy ways to reclaim yourself. Are there hobbies you gave up? Are there family members or friends you gave up? Are there dreams, callings, and steps of obedience you gave up? Reclaim them. For me, I began to use my prophetic gifting, spend more time with family and friends, and experience re-dreaming my future. During my marriage, I felt restrained, where I could not even make decisions for my own body. So, once we separated, I started dyeing my hair fun colors and I got eight ear piercings (I used to have eleven) because eight means new beginnings. I got contacts, new glasses, and even remodeled my room to reclaim my space. I also reclaimed my spiritual relationship with God as well as the authority He has given me and began to walk in His anointing. This was done through prayer and obedience to things/steps God gave me. I encourage you today to find out your lost dreams, giftings, ministries, relationships, and spiritual tools that God has given you. If you are unable due to trauma to remember what those were, ask God to bring them back to remembrance. Then begin to reclaim them in the ways God shows you as you pray. Remember when Jesus died on the cross, He took the keys. He took back the authority Satan had illegally obtained. Jesus is now calling to us, "Here are the *keys*, reclaim your *authority*, and be *restored*!"

Chapter 9:

What is God Saying?

"So, rise up, reclaim your present to grasp your future. A future that is beyond your imagination!"

I was thirteen when I truly committed my life to God and started my covenant relationship with Him. I remember it so very clearly. We were at a youth retreat and God just overwhelmed me. I knew I was loved and chosen by Him, that I was forgiven and set free from my old habits and ways of thinking. My life changed in one moment that set the course for the ministry and assignment God had given me. A couple of months later I was filled with the Holy Spirit and began speaking in tongues. Revelation after revelation came to me. God began speaking to me through dreams, the Bible, and through His Spirit to my spirit.

At nineteen, I went to a school that would allow me to have a greater experience in understanding other cultures, religions, and their need for Christ. I was beginning to really start digging deep into the giftings God had given me. It was while attending this school that I met my ex-husband. I thought that we would work the field together and that the ministry God was calling me to would change the world, yet one of the biggest assassinations I suffered during those fourteen years with him was to my calling and ministry. He constantly told me that I could not hear from God, and yet that was my calling. God told me at a very young age that He was calling me and anointing me as a prophet, to speak His words to the world, to both tear down and build up, and that He has a ministry for me. But during those fourteen years it was stolen from me; at times I laid it down just to survive, and at the end of it I felt dead. My relationship with God was barely surviving, my calling and purpose in life were taken away and I was trying to make sense of what my future held now. When God brought me out of the valley of death—and even before the change took place—I started reclaiming my relationship with God, my calling, and my giftings first. I came alive spiritually and began to walk in my authority from God, which allowed me to hear from God and make decisions that brought me into life.

A very exciting thing I learned was that God was not only healing me and restoring me, but He was also realigning me back to the original design He had for me. I want to share with you the words God spoke to me before the change and through the separation and divorce, and finally to what He is speaking today. However, I will also include some from 2007 through 2009 so we can see how God is realigning us to where we need to be. I feel very strongly in my spirit that these words from God are also for you. Let's jump in, and let the refreshing truth and hope allow us to take hold of our courage and stand firm!

December 31, 2020— Psalm 91; Doors will open.

January 4, 2021— Change is coming! I am in the midst! I am moving! Believe in Me! Press in and trust in ME! It is happening, things are moving into place BY MY SPIRIT!

January 9, 2021— Rest in Me; allow My peace to consume you. Do not run ahead, wait for My timing to be made perfect.

February 5, 2021— I know this is hard. You are going against everything you have come to believe about yourself and others. For so long you have believed their lies, accepted it in order to survive. I have chosen you. I am calling you to courageously break free and reclaim your title as My royal daughter/son. Stand your ground; you are valuable, treasured, wanted, and you are MINE. I will defend you; I will protect you, and I will set you FREE! I will set your feet on firm ground and take you into new directions. I will be your Father. I am calling you all back home as a family. Everything is happening fast, for I have sped up the timetable to protect you, and to bring things together sooner.

February 6, 2021— I have blessings that will be given during this time. I will provide for your every need. I will provide for you. I will show the world that you are blessed. You are highly favored and adored. I will defend your character, and all will know you belong to ME!

February 10, 2021— I know it seems slow, but it is happening quickly. I will bring truth out and will help you through the process. I will help make it easier, I will confirm you are making the right decision. I will be with you every step of the way. You will be cherished, loved, wanted, fought for, and you will have the desire of your heart fulfilled beyond your imagination.

February 23, 2021— Let it BEGIN!

March 4, 2021—You are not alone. I have never left you. I'm

holding you. Every tear that falls I have collected it. You are loved, I see you, and I know you. I have made a way out. Lean into Me for strength. It has already begun. Everything is moving into place. Stay in My presence so you can stay standing. Don't withdraw, don't flee, embrace it all, feel it all, and allow yourself to fully heal. I know it's painful, I know it hurts, I know you are scared, I know every thought, desire, and feeling you are experiencing. Answers to your questions will come at the right time. I know it's hard for you not to know what I know. Let Me do what needs to be done, and the time will come when you know what I know. I know you second guess yourself. You wonder if you are hearing Me clearly. Do not fear. Confirmation is coming. Confirmation is on the way. Fear not, but believe in Me.

March 6, 2021— It has begun. The wait is over. I am moving you to the next level. Justice, My justice, will prevail. I am calling you out. It's time for healing, freedom, and new beginnings. The old is gone and in its place, I am bringing new insight, new visions, and new dreams. I am calling you to new levels, new experiences, and a new path. The journey ahead will be hard, but what comes next is worth it. Isaiah 35.

March 24, 2021— Galatians 5:1 (NIV)- "It is for freedom that Christ has set us free. Stand firm, then, and do not let yourselves be burdened again by a yoke of slavery." I will answer your questions when the time is right. I will continue to give you each step. I am speaking. Your prayers are not being ignored. Hearts are softening to Me; lives are already changing. Watch and see how I answer. Don't forget that I have made things speed up. I am the God of the details.

March 26, 2021— My time is perfect. I am working all the details out. Doors will close and new doors will open to a bright future. Keep your eyes on Me. Don't lose focus, don't let fear hold you back, and don't lose faith. Remain in Me and at the end, you will remain standing.

April 6, 2021—I am the God of details. When everything comes out and comes together, you will understand.

April 11, 2021— What I have spoken, what I have promised, will come to pass. Keep your eyes open, for the sign and confirmation is on its way.

April 13, 2021— The tides are changing. A shift is taking place. There is a shaking in your life that will bring you closer to Me. Things have shifted in the spiritual realm, and soon it will begin to show in the physical realm. Claim your place. Claim your ministry. Claim your role in this family. Begin to walk it out spiritually. No man will be able to shut this door. I will honor you. I will bless and provide for you. Do not worry about money. I will provide for you. You will be My light in a dark world. Your life will bring Me honor and glory. When man tries to use your past to destroy you, I will use it to further My kingdom. I will use it for My honor and glory. Your pasts won't be a stumbling block but will help so many find freedom and healing. What I am doing has not just begun. We are in the middle of what I am doing. Soon the door will open.

April 14, 2021— This time needs to happen so you can step forward. This time is not a waste. You will not regret this time.

April 16, 2021—Psalm 32:7 (NIV)- "You are my hiding place; You will protect me from trouble and surround me with songs of deliverance."

April 17, 2021— Isaiah 30:18 (NIV) "Yet the LORD longs to be gracious to you; therefore he will rise up to show you compassion. For the LORD is a God of justice. Blessed are all who wait for him."

April 19, 2021— 1 Peter 1:13- (NIV) "Therefore, with minds that are alert and fully sober, set your hope on the grace to be brought to you when Jesus Christ is revealed at his coming." Habakkuk 2:2-3- (NIV) "Then the LORD replied: "Write down the revelation and make it plain on tablets so that a herald may run with it. For the revelation awaits an appointed time; it speaks of the end and it will not prove false. Though it linger, wait for it; it will certainly come and will not delay."

April 23, 2021— I will open the doors for you. This old season is ending, the door will be shut, and a new door will open. Revival will start. I will open a door that will take you in a new direction.

April 25, 2021— You are coming out from a time of wilderness wandering. Your next season will be full of refreshment, victories, and fulfillment. The door I open no man will be able to close. It is time to prepare and get yourself ready. Continue to take the steps needed for the old season to close and the new season to begin. Do not fear your past, what others think of you. You are loved. Do not fear but walk in who you are now, My royal daughter/son.

April 28, 2021— You have never truly been loved the way I have always wanted you to be loved. In these fifteen years you have not been loved, wanted, desired, treasured, cherished, protected, chosen, or put first (after Me). For fifteen years you have been a prisoner and slave. I am redeeming you, restoring you, and making Satan give back seven times what was stolen from you. You will be called blessed and favored.

May 25, 2021— 2 Kings 20:5- (NIV) "Go back and tell Hezekiah, the ruler of my people, 'This is what the LORD, the God of your father David, says: I have heard your prayer and seen your tears; I will heal you. On the third day from now you will go up to the temple of the LORD." Rebuild! Recover! Galatians 5:25- (NIV) "Since we live by the Spirit, let us keep in step with the Spirit." A new season is coming! A season of God-given blessings. A season like no other.

May 31, 2021— I am opening the Heavens. I am speaking to you.

I will reveal where you are at with Me. I am preparing for the door to open. My anointing will cover you all. I am about to do something miraculous in you and through you. I am breaking off every lie, deception, strongman, and stronghold. I am calling out, "Return, RETURN to ME!" I am about to do marvelous things. There will be no shame, embarrassment, or fear. My deep knowing and peace is flooding over you. I am about to give you a testimony that will glorify Me. Your life story will be like no one else's.

June 6, 2021— I will protect you. I will not reject you. Begin to believe Me right away without doubt. Love needs to have trust, not control. I will bless you. Continue to praise Me. I am moving you from first gear to fourth gear. You are on a cliff, ready for a new season. Obey Me, and follow Me. I am about to begin to show and reveal to you the coming season. You will be ready and prepared. You might not have all the details you want, but because of what I am teaching you, you will easily take each step-in faith. I will fulfill My promises. I am positioning you. Do not listen to the world, Satan is trying to cause fear and doubt. What the secular world sees is not being interpreted the right way. Declare what I give you to declare in the coming months. What you speak over yourself will destroy the enemy's plan and will protect you.

June 20, 2021— Ask the hard questions bravely.

June 26, 2021— The Word is coming. Heaven is opening and My words will fall like a heavy downpour. I am about to flood you with wisdom and understanding. My spirit will fall upon you, and you will see all I want you to see. Walls are about to break. The walls are about to break. I am awakening the heavens. The day for breakthrough is near. I am going to meet with you. I am going to speak with you. I will give you a voice.

June 27, 2021— I am removing distractions from off you. I am breaking down walls of bondage that have been a part of you for a long time. I am shifting your mindset. You will no longer call evil and sin good, nor righteousness and truth evil. You will receive healing, deliverance, and breakthrough, and your lives will change in just twenty-four hours. I am calling you into ministry for My kingdom. I have anointed you and equipped you. Satan, I say enough, release My sons and daughters. Today is your day for deliverance and breakthrough. When you wake up, you will see that things have changed. You will not be able to go back. I am getting you positioned before a new door. Walk, walk through. My words will be on your lips. I am touching your mouth, your tongue, and your mind.

July 9, 2021— The WAITING is OVER!

July 18, 2021— The winds have changed. The tide has shifted. I am about to position you for the new season. Satan has tried to kill this spiritual child (promises and calling) you are bearing. BUT this time you will birth the child. The child will be healthy, strong, and a blessing. Your new season is about to be birthed. You are laboring, you are pushing it forth with groans and deep pain. This season will be birthed at full term. Satan's attack has been stopped. I have placed new things in you. They have been growing and becoming stronger. They are ready to be birthed. You will not be stopped. There is a reason you were willing to let go of the abusive relationship for your calling and promises. I am birthing in you a new ministry, making your calling grow, and reminding you of who I am. Wondrous things are about to happen.

December 2021— You have a purpose and calling. I am not done with you. I am about to break through the stereotype and how people view you. I'm about to awaken the lion. It's time to roar. You do not need to strive to make it happen. You will walk into it. I have removed all restrictions from off you. The darkness has been too long, and it's time for My remnant to be blessed. Hope return, NOW! No longer will they or you be alone in a wilderness. This season was needed for them. I'm revealing things to them and putting them into place. You will understand the reasons, the why's soon. A double, a triple portion will be poured out on you. I am doing new things. The old is gone. The old wine skin has finished, it's time for the new. You laid down your calling, I will begin to open it up. Divine connections are going to take place. I will propel you forward. One connection will lead to another, till it leads you to who I have for you.

January 20, 2022— I am shining light on the path. This path will lead you through many doors. Keep your eyes open and in tune with Me. I am positioning you into your new role, where you will begin to use the authority I have given you. You will not be barren, but you will be fruitful.

February 2022— Today is the day of breakthrough. Today is the day where the strongman falls. Today is the day. Today is the day. I'm moving. I'm flooding over you. I'm flooding over you. Today is the day.

2007-2009

April 2007— You are not alone; you are never alone. I will never leave you. You are My joy. You are my desire. I am so proud of you. Your heart is on Me, your eyes are fixed on Me, and your ears are attuned to My voice. My blessings cover you. Claim your inheritance that I offer you. My words I place in your mouth, and My truth you will proclaim. I will lead you forth, I will call you forth to do My will. Though others may doubt you or question you, you will know without a doubt that what I speak, I mean. You will know My direction and My voice, you will know. Do not fear what the future holds, for I will give you strength. I will be your comfort. You are blessed and anointed by Me. I am with you.

April 21, 2007— Do not worry, I have a plan. I have something great in mind. Trust Me, I am taking care of it. I have a plan and soon you will see it. I have kept you in the dark, but soon your eyes will be open, and My light will shine through. The time is drawing close, you will soon be in a new place.

May 8, 2007—Purify yourself. Guard your mind. Keep a right mindset. 1 Corinthians 7:3-5.

May 10, 2007— Your birthing pains have begun. You will begin to have contractions. Do not be scared, do not let fear hold you from this birth. This spiritual baby is a blessing to you. It will be painful to birth, but you will experience My joy and grace through it.

August 2007— My shaking has begun. Now things are set in motion. Things have begun. I am beginning to fulfill My promises. They are starting to come to fulfillment. You are ready.

August 25, 2007— You feel like you are in a place of death or brokenness. You want to know what I am doing, what My plan is for you. Psalm 118, Psalm 18. You feel as though you are dying, but I will not let death have a hold over you. You will live and be strong. You will be victorious and out of your mouth I will speak. I will use you. I will not let you remain in this place.

August 26, 2007— You are in a furnace. I have upped the flames. Many cannot handle this temperature, but I made you and I know you can stand the fire. Though you feel like you are burning alive, you will not die. Daniel 3. Although the fire is hotter and deadlier to your flesh, I am still with you. I am walking beside you. You will be sent. Continue to be diligent in the goal of being sent out.

Prepare yourself now, do things to get ready to be sent. Do not say the time is too long, for it is shorter than you realize.

September 16, 2007— Become refreshed! Soak in My presence, allow all the worry, all your fears to fall away. Drink of My presence. I want to heal your heart, heal your emotions, and heal your body. I want to set you free. I want to make you mature in Me. I want you to surrender so I can fully use you. Soak in Me. Open yourself up to Me. I want to take away all the fears that hold you back from Me.

September 25, 2007— There is a testimony just for you. A testimony I have created for you, to glorify Me. I know this is hard, I know it's not what you expected, or even wanted to go through. Do not be discouraged, be strong. You will be confident in what I have promised.

October 14, 2007— Out of the belly flows life. Psalm 92. You are a testimony of My love, compassion, and My strength. You have done things that most people could not have survived. You became a pillar, beautifully carved from trials, persecution, tests, and perseverance. You have become a strength to others. Look back a year ago and you will see that you are no longer the same. You have matured and have gone after My heart. I know you are tired of always being strong. I know you suffer in silence. I know the pain is unbearable, and you cry and weep like a woman travailing in childbirth. I am so proud of you. Because of your sacrifice things will change; because you give all of yourself things will not remain this way. Chains are broken off; bondages and strongmen are all destroyed. Freedom reigns in your life. You speak the truth and every day you have learned how to speak in love. You have walked a hard path, a hard life. Misunderstandings happen because people are still learning who you are. You need to release your past and forgive them. Release them from all the pain and hurt they caused you. Set them free, let go and let Me come and completely heal your heart. Trust in Me. See My glory in your life. It's time to move on into your future and let the past go. I want to do amazing things in your life. I want to take you places that need you, that cry out for you. You have learned to be weak with Me. You have learned how to love. You have learned how to trust. You have learned how to seek Me. You obey with a willing heart; you follow Me no matter how hard. You do not allow fear or pain to stop you. You know how to love others, how to place them above yourself. I am so proud of you. You glorify and praise Me. Every step you take, I am there with you. Every step you will know. I have given you the keys to the kingdom.

October 23, 2007—I have given you keys and with those keys power is given. I am going to train you in how to use this power for My glory. (A word from my dad: You are in a season of preparation for the future and what I have already spoken to you about. Step out in faith.) Hold on to Me, I am opening doors. I will make a way where there seems to be no way. You will see. The time is now. I will make a way. The door is open. Watch and see, you will see My glory, My sign of faithfulness. Watch and see Me move. It will work out. Trust. Do not be afraid of what power that is within you or even that when you pray nothing happens. For it is spiritual, you have created damage against your enemy.

April 20, 2008— My grace is enough. My love covers, forgives, cleans, and protects you. I'm restoring back what Satan stole away. I am giving you your freedom, joy, hope, love, dreams, callings, and your promises that I have given to you. I am going to give back all that Satan stole and give you a double portion. My blessings are going to flood you, and all will see I am God and I make all things new. I am the God who restores. Never forget you are My child. My will is good and holy. It is a wonderful plan for your life. I am using you to show grace, forgiveness, and love. The things you are overcoming are making you stronger. It is making your foundation strong and holy. It will glorify Me. I trust you, I know your heart, and I know what is best for you.

August 25, 2008— I can work all things out for My glory. That which seems impossible to you is possible for Me. I have set you free. This is a new day, a new season in your life. Change, lots of changes. This is our journey. This is our path that we shall walk together.

October 8, 2008— Psalm 92, Isaiah 49, Psalm 99. I have not changed My will. The promises I gave you still stand. I am leading you in peace and joy. Put your trust in Me, and I will lead you in My truth. You are becoming the woman/man I created you to be. You are so beautiful. I created you in My image. I made you. I see the good in you. I see, I know. I know the things you struggle with, but I see the change in you. Before you were weak and easily swayed by the world, but now you fight for your purity, for your righteousness, and you don't give in. I speak healing over your body, heart, and mind. My love covers you. My peace I pour out on you. My blood covers you. You are My bride clothed in white. Clothed in beauty and righteousness. You are royalty. I forgive you, and you need to forgive yourself. I know you hurt because of your choices. You have made things right; you are forgiven and free. Release it, release it all to Me. The process is an amazing thing. It takes time, but if done according to My will it turns into something beautiful and pure. I have protected you. Your past is erased. Yes, you still have memories, but I have reversed it. I have restored you. I am God, who has the power. I am changing it and making things new.

October 15, 2008— I am making My ways your ways. My thoughts I place in your mind. I will use you to bring light to the world. I will use you to bring healing to My children. I am changing your mindset. I am creating a new attitude. Sing, pray, act in the opposite spirit, praise Me. Get away for a time and soak in My presence. Call out to Me and I will help you. I will speak truth into the situation.

December 31, 2008— A new season has begun for you. You are in a new place, a new level of intimacy. You have walked through the valley of death, and our testimony has been strengthened. You have turned away from Me and now you have returned. You have been led into freedom. Depression, darkness, and pain were once your companion, but now joy, peace, and I are your companion. The last year you have faced fears, failures, and immaturity. You have grown so much. Your foundation has become strong and sure. You are in a new place. This coming year many things will change. The old things will fall away, and new things will continue to grow. Promises will be fulfilled. Deliverance will come. Relationships will come. You have been tested and tried. In your weaknesses and failures, you held through and allowed them to bring you closer to Me. In this coming year prayers will be answered. Promises will be fulfilled. My will, will be done. It has been a long process to get you to where you are at. A lot of lessons had to be learned. Many heart issues had to be overcome, circumcision of your heart had to take place. My faithfulness has proven true. Everything I spoke will be done. This coming year will be full of blessings. Seek Me for each step and I will lead you. Trust Me.

January 30, 2009— Daniel 2: 20-23. Listen, My child, for this is what is in My heart. Wisdom and might are Mine. I change the times and the seasons. I remove kings and raise up kings. I give wisdom to the wise and knowledge to those who have understanding. I reveal deep and secret things. I know what is in the darkness, and light dwells in Me. I have given you wisdom and might. I have made known to you that which you have asked. All things will work out for My glory.

August 15, 2009— Your prayers do change things. You have been disappointed by man many times, and you tend to think I will do the same to you. People tried to encourage you, but they said the wrong thing and it made you question yourself. You feel that I will still punish you for when you sin. You question if I truly forgive you, and if your punishment is really over. You are extreme with what you feel. You are high and low. You have a hard time finding a balance. You knew you could trust Me and that is why your hope was high. This is why you kept praying. But after a time, you doubted yourself, you doubted if I could really love you. You question why I would bless you, you began to look at your mistakes instead of remembering that I chose to bless you, because I love you. You were in a battle, a test, and you can learn so much from this. Do not feel like you failed Me, because I am using this to show you things, to build you up, and to make your path straight. A lot of your questions are based on your doubts. Sometimes you will get hurt, but you must trust that I have a plan. I do not expect you to rejoice when that happens. I know you will feel hurt, angry, sad, disappointed, and so on. But it's like your dad said, "the outcome is up to you." What are you going to do with your feelings? Are you going to run away from Me? You can get easily depressed when you go through something big. You opened a door for Satan, and he now knows your weaknesses, but when you are aware of it, you know how to fight against it. It was easy, every step was a piece of cake. It all went smoothly, we had no problems, because I did a miracle. But you took your eyes off truth and doubted Me and yourself. You didn't see the bigger picture, BUT you need to stand in Me. You know Me, we have relationship. Do not ever forget that I love you. And even if things do not turn out the way you expected, know that I see your obedience. I see you.

October 4, 2009— Do not be afraid, little warrior bride, victory is on the other side. You are not alone. Do you believe that because of your past that I consider you lower than those around you? Do you believe that My love changes? Or do you believe that My love is always love and I love everyone? I do not have a list or a record of your wrongs. Do not let the judgment of man cloud your views of who I am. I am not man, I am God. My salvation is for everyone.

• • •

It was not until after my divorce was finalized that God told me to go back and read my journal from 2007-2009. I questioned God about why, because I knew there would be things in there concerning memories and areas of hurt with my ex-husband. But as I obeyed, He opened my eyes to His amazing love for me. I saw that He still had a plan and a purpose for me, my life was not over, and He was taking me back to where I was then. It showed me that although years have passed, God is restoring me and that I am stepping into what He designed for me long ago. As I was writing this chapter I prayed and asked God if there was anything He wanted me to share in closing this chapter. Here is what He gave me.

February 27, 2022

Today is the day to say YES to Me. Put aside your fears, doubts, and need to be in control. You need to come to this understanding, you will never have all the understanding of Me, and yet as you say yes to a covenant relationship with Me, I will reveal Myself to you more and more. Step out in faith, believe that I will heal you. Let go of the victim mentality, the need to remain where you are. I have created you, and you have so much more than this death. I have a fulfilling, blessed, and anointed purpose and calling on your life. You are meant to be free, loved, and prosperous. Today meet with Me, surrender yourself to Me, and begin to forgive and repent. When you choose Me and are obedient to Me, I will radically change your life and in a very short time you will find yourself in a new place. The old will be gone and you will be walking in FREEDOM and RESTORATION. I want to realign you and bring you back to your original design. Release it all to Me. Release your anger, resentment, pain, and past. Let us walk this new path together. You will not be alone. If you look for Me each day you will see Me and how I am moving in your life. Today, today is the day for your VICTORY! Claim your future. Reclaim yourself, your promises, your ministry, your hopes, and dreams. Reclaim! Stand Firm! Be bold! Activate your courage! Let's go! LET IT BEGIN!

Chapter 10:

What Are My New Perspectives

and Views Now?

Joshua 1:9 (NIV)- "Have I not commanded you? Be strong and courageous. Do not be afraid; do not be discouraged, for the Lord your God will be with you wherever you go."

Abuse, trauma, and PTSD have given me the awesome privilege of understanding myself and God in a way that is very personal to me. I do not wish what I have been through on anyone, and I am sure that you feel the same way about your story, but I love that God can redeem those areas and make them beautiful. I know that may sound crazy, and if you are not at a certain level of healing you might even find that offensive. But when you reach the end, you will also see the power of God at work throughout it all. I feel great joy and peace knowing that He has always been with me and that I was chosen and loved long ago. I wanted to share with you some of the ways that my perspective has changed after everything I've been through, for you to see, understand, and join me in living a life out of the box for God. I realized that before and during my story, I had always put God in a box and limited the power and miracles He could do in my life. This year though, God has completely removed Himself from my box, taken hold of my hand, and together we are walking on an uncharted path that is daring, extreme, and led by the Holy Spirit.

Where is God and why is so there so much evil around me?

I have heard over and over people asking if there is a God, and if He is real, why does He allow all these bad things? I want to take time to address some areas, because my trauma and abuse gave me some very clear understanding on the answer. Yes, there is a God. He is real and He is alive. Jesus died on the cross for my sins and rose again so I can be made whole and have fellowship with God. The Holy Spirit is active and around us.

My situation showed me Satan was real, that wickedness is also around us and trying to snare us. The demonic agenda Satan has planned is real and being acted upon. There is evil and darkness here on earth, active in the hearts of those who live in flesh apart from God.

We are all sinners, yet Christ came for us. Daily we choose who we will serve— God or Satan. So why does God allow bad things to happen? God is good and there is no sin or evil in Him. He is perfect and He stands by His Word. He gave us this world to govern and rule, not over each other, but everything else. Yet sin entered the scene and Satan took our authority illegally and we were separated from God. Christ came, died on the cross, and rose again. He gave us back our authority, but we get to choose if we will use it. What does that have to do with God allowing bad things to happen? God is love, and He does not abuse us.

God gave mankind a choice to be in a relationship with Him or choose ourselves and Satan. John 14:6 says, "Jesus answered, 'I am the way and the truth and the life. No one comes to the father except through me." We have two options, that is it! God will not force us to be with Him. He will not take away the authority He gave us to govern earth. Until the believers leave this world, it is ours. He has given us freewill. Do you know how powerful and loving that is? As someone who spent fourteen years being manipulated, controlled, and forced to abide, I can feel the love and freedom this knowledge brings. I cannot even think about going back into that abusive situation, and there is freedom in knowing God will never force me in our relationship. He longs for us to choose Him and righteousness, because of our love for Him. He wants a true relationship with us, not a fake one. He longs for us to experience good things, His love and forgiveness, and to live in His presence.

Why, then, is there wickedness, evil, chaos, and darkness? Because the consequence of God giving us freewill means man can choose to sin. For there to be only good and the earth to be healthy, God would need to control and force everyone on earth to choose Him and then redeem the world, and we would never get our freewill back.

What happens when a child does something wrong, but is never disciplined? The child continues in his behaviors until it leads to his destruction. When a child is disciplined and changes, he has a better chance to bring good to the world. God also disciplines His children in love. There are natural consequences to our choices. Good also has good consequences. Our choices affect others around us; if we are not corrected, we will continue in our ways. What is a natural consequence for my ex-husband not changing? He lost me. He lost what I brought into his life, and we will be separated for the rest of our earthly life. There is fear, violence, sickness, murder, etc., because sin entered the world, and we have freewill. The world remains in a fallen state until Jesus returns to reclaim the earth. I believe that what we experience on earth breaks God's heart, because this is never what He intended for us. Because of this, He sent His son to redeem us, and one day He will send Jesus again to bring us out of this fallen world and into goodness with Him.

We must remain here for now because He will not abuse us and take away our choices and freewill. However, we can still live in goodness, joy, health, blessings, and favor by having a covenant relationship with Him and remaining in Him on this earth. Trust me, there is a God, and He is so good and loving. My freewill is a glaring fact that this is true. Bad things do happen, and we can sit around trying to figure out why, or we can trust God. Even through my worst traumas I still see how God was with me and protecting me. We will never truly understand the reason for why things happen to the innocent, not until we get to heaven. The main thing is that we are not God; in our own minds, we are unable to comprehend how to love everyone on this earth and not go against freewill. We must choose to trust and rest without knowing. For some people that will be easier said than done, but I encourage everyone to begin to walk in trust in God.

What to do when our promises involve others?

This is a hard one. Whether it has to do with a spouse, family, friend, or ministry, our promises do not change, yet because everyone has freewill the people involved in the promises can change. If I fail to do what God has called me to, He will bring someone else to fulfill it. If you have someone you are waiting on as a future spouse, but he/she fails to obey God, God will bring another into your life. It can be hard to come to terms with that, but it also strengthens my resolve to be obedient and right with God, so I do not miss out on my role in other peoples' promises, and experience fulfillment in promises for myself and others. It also pushes me to encourage others to do the same.

How do I view my future?

I view my future with hope. I went through horrible moments in my past, but because I am free and healed the future is bright. I do not let anything steal that hope. Yes, the end of ends described in the book of Revelation will come someday, but instead of being afraid or throwing up my arms and saying, "Take me now," I see what God wants to do in my life each day. Ask yourself: who does He want me to speak to? Where does He want me to go? And then recognize the divine connections. He will fulfill every promise and calling because He is faithful. The end times will not stop that; tribulation, persecution, or anything else we will face will not stop where God wants us, who we are to meet, and the promises and callings on our lives. We will get to see God do miracles straight out of the New Testament. Let go of fear, worry, anxiety, or anything else that will drain your hope and peace. God is still God, and He never lies.

As the world gets darker and darker, what should my perspective be?

We need to stop saying, "This is how it will always be. Take us now, God." God is not done with us. We have a calling upon our lives. What we have been through and experienced, God is going to use to help others. Stop believing and proclaiming negativity, lies, and hopelessness over yourself and the calling God gave you. Begin to proclaim truth and hope, reminding yourself of God's promises over you, the vision and calling He has shown you for your life. Get out of unbelief and stand firm in faith.

Ending Thoughts

God is calling you to move out of where you are at right now. Open your eyes and ears to Him. I can guarantee that when you walk in covenant relationship with Him, obey Him, and heal, by this time next year you will not be the same or in the same place.

I am not the same. I am healed. I am whole. I am not the same.

So, rise up, reclaim your present to grasp your future. A future that is beyond your imagination!

Joshua 1:9 (NIV)- "Have I not commanded you? Be strong and courageous. Do not be afraid; do not be discouraged, for the Lord your God will be with you wherever you go."

References

"Common Responses to High Stress and/or Trauma." 2016. Eastern Mennonite University. https://emu.edu/cjp/star/docs/Common_Responses.pdf.

Domestic Shelters. "Withholding Intimacy Can Be Abusive Too." August 30, 2017. https://www.domesticshelters.org/articles/identifying-abuse/withholding-intimacy-can-be-abusive-too.

Mayo Clinic. Post-traumatic Stress Disorder (PTSD). 2022 Mayo Foundation for Medical Education and Research (MFMER). https://www.mayoclinic.org/diseases-conditions/post-traumatic-stress-disorder/symptoms-causes/syc-20355967.

MOBIEG. "Adult Grooming." August 15, 2021. https://www.mobieg.co.za/abuse/adult-grooming/.

National Adult Protective Services Association. "What is Abuse?" NAPSA. 2022. https://www.napsa-now.org/get-informed/what-is-abuse/.

National Domestic Violence Hotline. "What is Spiritual Abuse?" National Domestic Violence Hotline. https://www.thehotline.org/resources/what-is-spiritual-abuse/.

Jim Norman. 2016 Eastern Mennonite University. http://www.emu.edu/star

Stines, Sharie. "Emotional Abuse and Threats of Abandonment." December 19, 2017. https://psychcentral.com/pro/recovery-expert/2017/12/emotional-abuse-and-threats-of-abandonment#1.

Trails to Wellness. "5 Fs of Trauma Response." 2013. The Regents of the University of Michigan. TRAILStoWellness.org.

Women's Rural Resource Center. "Abuse and Manipulation Tactics." https://wrrcsa.org/education/how-to-hide-your-tracks-online/

Author Contact

If you would like to have Aubrey Dawn Weinzetl come and speak at a Bible Study, conference, event, etc., want to know when her next book will come out, hear about opportunities to hear her in person and the events she will be doing; please visit her at:

Website: **www.aubreydw.com**

Facebook: **https://www.facebook.com/AubreyDawnWeinzetl**

Email: **Aubrey.heldhostage@gmail.com**